How to use this book

Follow the advice, in italics, given for you on each page.
Praise *the children at every step!*

Detailed guidance is provided in the Read Write Inc. Phonics Handbook.

7 reading activities

Children:

☆ *Practise reading the speed sounds.*

☆ *Read the green and red words for the Ditty.*

☆ *Listen as you read the introduction.*

☆ *Read the Ditty.*

☆ *Re-read the Ditty and discuss the 'questions to talk about'.*

☆ *Re-read the Ditty with fluency and expression.*

☆ *Practise reading the speed words.*

G000162090

Speed Sounds

Consonants

Say the pure sounds (do not add 'uh').

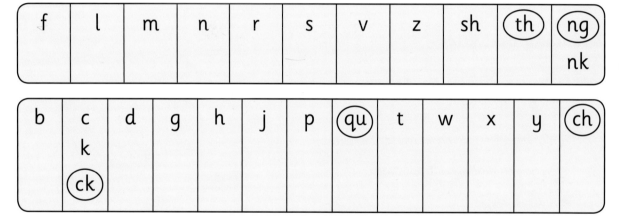

f	l	m	n	r	s	v	z	sh	(th)	(ng)
										nk

b	c	d	g	h	j	p	(qu)	t	w	x	y	(ch)
	k											
	(ck)											

Vowels

Say the sounds in and out of order.

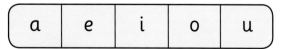

a	e	i	o	u

Each box contains only one sound. Focus sounds are circled.

Ditty 1 # Let's sing

Green words

Read in Fred Talk (pure sounds).

can dog frog si<u>ng</u>

<u>ch</u>i<u>ck</u> du<u>ck</u> so<u>ng</u> a

Read the root word first and then with the ending.

let → let's

Red words

<u>th</u>e

Ditty 1 # Let's sing

Introduction

Do you like singing? In this story lots of animals have fun singing.

the frog can sing

the duck can sing

the dog can sing

the chick can sing

let's sing a song

Ditty 2   Kiss Kiss

Green words

Read in Fred Talk (pure sounds).

cot   ki<u>ss</u>   rug   wi<u>th</u>   du<u>ck</u>

ba<u>th</u>   in   <u>qu</u>a<u>ck</u>   on   his

Red words

<u>th</u>e

Ditty 2 Kiss kiss

Introduction

Do you have a younger brother or sister? In this story we meet a baby.
Let's see what he likes doing.

on <u>the</u> rug

ma-ma

in the bath with his duck

quack quack

in his cot

ki<u>ss</u> ki<u>ss</u>

Ditty 3   La-la-la

Green words

Read in Fred Talk (pure sounds).

can   ba**ng**   drum   si**ng**
wi**th**   band

Read the root word first and then with the ending.

lot → lots   so**ng** → so**ng**s

Red words

I   **th**e   of

La-la-la

I can bang the drum

bang bang

I can sing lots of songs

la-la-la

I can si<u>ng</u> with <u>the</u> band

Questions to talk about

Ditty 1

Which animal sings first?

What do the animals do at the end of the story?

What song shall we sing?

Ditty 2

What does the baby have with him in the bath?

What does Mum do before the baby goes to sleep?

What do you like doing at bathtime / bedtime?

Ditty 3

What instrument can the girl play?

What does the girl do in the band?

What musical instrument would you like to play in a band?

Speed words for Ditty 1

Children practise reading the words across the rows, down the columns and in and out of order clearly and quickly.

can	dog	frog	sing
chick	duck	song	a

Speed words for Ditty 2

cot	on	kiss	the
duck	with	bath	in

Speed words for Ditty 3

can	I	bang	drum
song	with	of	sing